T0161437

Between the Floating Mist

Between the Floating Mist

POEMS OF RYŌKAN

Translated by Dennis Maloney & Hide Oshiro

WHITE PINE PRESS / BUFFALO, NEW YORK

Published by
White Pine Press
P.O. Box 236
Buffalo, NY 14201
www.whitepine.org

Acknowledgements: Portions of Section One, "Between the Floating Mist," and all of section three, "Dewdrops on a Lotus Leaf," originally appeared in *Between the Floating Mist* (Buffalo, NY, Springhouse Editions, 1992). Section Two appeared originally as *I Pass Through This World*, a chapbook published by Longhouse Editions, Green River, Vermont in early 2009.)

Publication of this book was made possible, in part, with funds from the New York State Council on the Arts.

Cover image: Shiro Kasamatsu (1898–1991) *Evening Rain at Shinobazu Park*

First Edition

ISBN 978-1-935210-05-4

Printed and bound in the United States of America

Library of Congress Control Number: 2009920563

Dedicated to the memory of the poet and traveler
Nanao Sakaki
who showed us it was possible
to live this life of Ryōkan in the 21st century

and to

Edith Shiffert and Akio Saito

Contents

Introduction / 9

Between the Floating Mist / 15

I Pass Through This World / 37

Dewdrops on a Lotus Leaf / 57

Introduction

Taigu Ryōkan (1758-1831) was a Zen monk of the Soto sect. A poet, master calligrapher, and hermit; he is one of the most beloved poets of Japan. Taking the name Daigu or "Great Fool," he was often seen playing games with the village children or begging for food throughout town.

Born in 1758 in the village of Izumozaki in Echigo province (present-day Niigata prefecture in the north of Honshu, the main island of Japan), Ryōkan entered the monastery at age seventeen. His father was the headman of the village and a haiku poet. As the eldest son, Ryōkan would have inherited his father's post had he not become a monk.

In 1779 he became a disciple of the Zen master Kokusen and studied with him for over ten years at Entsuji. He received *Inka* (recognition for his enlightenment) from Kokusen and became a Zen master in his own right. After the death of Kokusen in 1791, he left Entsuji and wandered for five years as an *Unsui* (cloud and water) monk, drifting from place to place.

Instead of becoming the head of a Zen temple as many Zen masters did, Ryōkan preferred the simple and independent life of a hermit. In 1804 he settled in a one-room hut on the slopes of Mt. Kugami, where he stayed for thirteen years. Although he lived as a hermit, Ryōkan was hardly a recluse. Rather than remaining in the confines of the temple, as the tenth Oxherding Picture suggests, he returned to the marketplace and the world. He often came to nearby villages to visits friends, play with the children, and beg for food in the Buddhist tradition.

Ryōkan's poetry is simple, direct, and colloquial in expression. His work shows the influence of the Chinese poet recluse Han Shan, whose work he admired, and that of Saigyo, the 12th century Japanese poet and monk. Ryōkan's poetry and his life are inseparable. Many of his poems are about the seasons, playing with the village children and records of his daily activities, including snow-bound winters, gathering firewood and plants, begging trips, and meditation on Buddhist themes.

Ryōkan wrote poetry in Japanese and, as was customary of Buddhist priests, in Chinese. The first section of the book, "Between the Floating Mist," is a selection of Ryōkan's *kanshi* poems written in Chinese. The poems in the second section,

"I Pass Through This World," are a selection of *tanka* written by Ryōkan in Japanese. In 1826, when he was 68, Ryōkan became friends with Teishin, a Buddhist nun forty years his junior. The two exchanged numerous poems, creating a unique poetic dialog, which is collected in the third section of the book, "Dewdrops On a Lotus Leaf." Teishin compiled this collection under this title after Ryōkan's death.

The Mt. Kugami area suffered severe winters and Ryōkan was often snowed in during the winter months. During these periods he read the Chinese and Japanese classics including Han-Shan, Su tung-po, and the *Man'yoshu*. When age made it difficult for him to hike up and down the mountain, he moved to a hut on the grounds of Otogo Shrine at the foot of the mountain and later to a renovated storehouse at the home of a friend in the village of Shimazaki. "Dewdrops On a Lotus Leaf" records the last years of his life up to his death in 1831 at seventy-three years of age. Ryōkan left behind in his poetry the essence of the Zen life:

> What shall remain
> as my legacy?
> The spring flowers,
> the cuckoo in summer,
> the autumn leaves.

Section 1

Between the Floating Mist

Firewood bundled on my shoulders, I descend
a steep path down the green mountain.
Occasionally I rest awhile under a tall pine,
listening quietly to the spring birds sing.

Listening to the silence
of a moss covered stream
I grow calm and transparent,
still as the motionless current.

Living alone in the woods,
few visitors cast shadows.
How clean the moon
gleaming in the sky.

At Saito's Country House

A few miles from town
I walk with a woodcutter,
Pines line the roadside.
From the other side of the valley
a fragrant wind of plum blossoms.
Arriving here, I feel at home.
Koi swim in an old pond,
the forest quiet on a spring day.
What's in this room?
A few books of poetry on the table.
At ease, I loosen my belt,
select some phrases and try to write a poem.
At dusk I go outside to stroll
and a startled quail flies across the sky.

Along the mossy path misty flowers bloom,
mystic birds weave sounds into songs.
The spring day slowly graces my window.
A thin line of smoke rises straight up from the hearth.

How long has it been since
the teaching of the pure essence was swept away?
Students are caught up with the written word
and Buddhist priests are stubbornly obsessed with doctrine.
It's a shame that for a thousand years
no one has spoken seriously of this essence.
Better to follow the children and bounce a ball
on these spring days.

I remember my days at Entsu-ji
and my struggle along the way.
Collecting firewood reminds me of layman Pang,
and pounding rice, the sixth patriarch.
I was among the first to meet my teacher
and spent hours in meditation.
Thirty years have passed
since I left the temple.
With mountains and seas between us
I hear no news,
but I will never forget my teacher's kindness.
My tears flow, blending with this stream.

I'm truly simple
living among trees and grasses.
Don't ask me about illusion or enlightenment.
I'm just an old man who smiles to himself.
I ford streams with these thin legs,
and carry my bag in fine weather.
Such is my life,
but the world owes me nothing.

As a boy I learned the classics
but was too lazy to become a Confucian.
As a young man I chased after zen,
but gained no Dharma worth passing on.
Now I live in a hut by a Shinto shrine
and work as the custodian,
sometimes caretaker, sometimes monk.

Girls gathering lotus, sing a pleasant song.
Their fresh make-up reflects clear in the water.
Offshore white waves rise like a mountain,
and the sailboats rush back toward the cove.

Grass for a pillow, I slept in the fields
and heard nothing but lonely birds chirping.
Both nobles and peasants are nothing
but a single night's dream.

After begging food around town
I proudly return carrying my bag.
Returning where? Do you know?
To my home in the white clouds.

The tall banana trees in front of my window
sweep the clouds cool.
Reading and composing poems
I sit surrounded by them all day long.

Ever since I embraced the way
I've cared little for things of this world,
leaving destiny to chance.
In my bag three measures of rice
and by the hearth a bundle of firewood.
Why worry about salvation or karma?
Fortune and fame are only so much dust!
On a rainy night, I stretch out
my legs and fall asleep.
My dwelling, a tiny hut in the woods.

Who says my poem is poem?
My poem, in fact, is not poem.
When you realize that my poem is not poem,
then we can discuss poetry.

The song of cicadas in the branches,
the voice of water under rocks.
Rain last night washed away the soot and dust.
Don't say there's nothing special in my grass hut.
Come and I'll share with you a window full of cool air.

In my hand I carry a hare-horn cane,
around my body I wear a robe of illusory flowers,
and on my feet shoes of knitted tortoise hair.
My mouth chants a soundless poem.

I watch a teacher lecture on the sutras
His eloquence flows like running water.
Expounding on the five stages and the eight categories,
he explains them with unequaled cleverness.
They proclaim themselves masters
and others believe it.
However, question them about the essence of Zen
and they have no useful answer.

Evening meditation, enfolded in mountains,
all thoughts of the world of men dissolve.
Quietly sitting on my cattail cushion
alone, I face the empty window.
Incense burns away as the dark night deepens,
and my robe is a single fold, as white dew thickens.
Rising from deep meditation, I stroll in the garden,
and the moon is already above the highest peak.

A single path through a dense forest,
mountains peek out from between the floating mist.
Not yet autumn, the leaves have already disappeared
and without rain the rocks are always dark.
I gather the tree mushrooms in a basket
and draw spring water into a jar.
Except for a stray traveler
no one finds the way here.
The water of the mind, how clear it is!

Gazing at it, the boundaries are invisible.
But as soon as even a slight thought arises,
ten thousand images crowd it.
Attach to them and they become real;
be carried by them and it will be difficult to return.
How painful to see a person trapped in the ten-fold delusions.

Day after day, day in and day out,
·I spend my life leisurely, in the company of children,
with a few balls up my sleeve,
a useless fellow drunk on the peace of spring.

Rags and tatters, torn and tattered,
rags and tatters, such is my life.
Sustenance, I beg for it along the road.
My hut, overgrown with weeds.
Moon watching, I spend the night chanting poems.
Lost in blossoms, I forget to go home.
Since I left the temple of my teacher,
such is the life I lead.

Dialogue in a Dream

Begging food, I went to the village.
On the road I met a wise old teacher.
He asked, "Monk, why are you living
among the white shrouded peaks?"
In return I asked him, "Why are you
growing old in the midst of the city's dust?"
We were each about to answer, but neither had
spoken before the bell shattered my dream.

A ball in my sleeve more valuable than gold.
To my skill there is no equal.
If you ask what I mean,
I reply 1, 2, 3, 4, 5, 6, 7, …

The flower does not invite the butterfly,
and the butterfly has no intention of visiting the flower.
But when flowers bloom the butterfly comes
and when the butterfly comes flowers bloom.
I don't know those others,
and they don't know me, either,
but we are all followers of the Way.

A quiet night behind my grass hut.
Alone, I play a stringless lute.
Its melody drifts to the wind-blown clouds and fades.
Its sound deepens with the running stream,
expanding till it fills a deep ravine
and echoes through the vast woods.
Who, other than a deaf person, can hear this faint song?

In my hut a copy of Han-shan's poems.
They are better than any sutra.
I copy his poems and post them,
enjoying each one again and again.

Surrounded by green mountains,
white clouds left and right.
If I meet a fellow traveler
what news can I give him?

Wandering alone in the mountains
I discover my old abandoned hut:
crumbling walls, animal tracks,
a dry well next to an old bamboo grove.
Webs cover the window where I once read.
Layers of dust cover the floor,
and stairs are hidden by wild grasses.
Disturbed, crickets chirp.
I can hardly bear to leave,
looking up at the setting sun.

It is fine to see young people
stay home and enthusiastically compose poems,
imitating the classic styles of the Han and Wei
and mastering the contemporary styles of the Tang.
Although their style is excellent, even novel,
unless the poem says something from the inner heart
what shall we do with so many empty words?

Alone at night in my solitary mountain hut,
snow brings on lonesome thoughts.
A mysterious monkey cry echoes on the peak.
The stream in the ravine, frozen silent.
The water in the inkstone by my pillow has dried,
and the lamplight is still by the window.
The night is uneasy and I can't sleep.
Warming my brush with my breath,
I try to compose a poem.

Looking back on over seventy years, I tire
of seeing through the right and wrong of the world of man.
The path outside shows no footprints in the late night snow,
a stick of incense burning in front of the window.

After begging food all day
I return home, shut the rough wood door,
and burn leaves and twigs in the hearth,
quietly chanting Han-shan's poems.
Night, the rainy west wind blows,
rustling the thatched roof.
Meanwhile, I stretch out my legs and lie down,
pondering what should I think about, what should I doubt?

A thousand mountain peaks, a frozen mass of snow.
Ten thousand mountain paths without human trace.
Everyday I sit facing the wall.
Occasionally I hear snow pounding the window.

For an old man, a dream is easily broken.
Waking, I enter the empty room
lit by an oil lamp, but soon
the lamp is exhausted leaving the long winter night.

Confined to my snow covered hut
on the slope of Mt. Kugami,
no one visits.
Snowing night and day.
Humans leave no trace,
not even a shadow.
Only a thin mountain stream
flowing among the rocks
like a straw rope sustains me.

Spare, my three-mat room,
a wreck, this old body of mine.
In these long winter months
I have trouble talking about all my ills.
Sipping thin soup, I make it through the night
And patiently wait for spring.
If I don't beg for a measure of rice,
how will I make it through the winter?
Contemplating, I don't come up with a plan,
so I send you this poem, my friend.

I Pass Through the World

Spring

They tell me
spring has arrived
but the sky is misty.
On the mountain
no flowers, only snow.

Spring awakens
with blossoming plum trees.
But now falling petals
mix with
the brush warbler's song.

In the garden—just us
a plum tree
in full blossom
and this old man
long in years.

The spring birds
have returned.
Songs drift
from tree to tree
—pour another cup of sake.

Tonight, plum blossoms
reflect a silver moon,
both in full bloom.
Enchanted I don't
return home until after midnight.

I traveled to this village
to view the plum blossoms
but distracted spend the day
looking at flowers
along the river bank.

Thirsty, I take
my fill of sake.
Lying under
cherry blossoms
—what splendid dreams!

At last spring
has arrived.
Under trees
by this shrine
I play with children.

I think snowflakes
are blurring
the entire sky,
but it's a shower
of falling cherry blossoms.

What pleasure
I feel these
spring days
seeing birds flit
about in joyous play.

With gifts of
seaweed, sake,
and daikon
my spring won't
be so lonely.

What shall remain
as my legacy?
The spring flowers,
the cuckoo in summer,
the autumn leaves.

Summer

Picking violets
along the road,
I forgot my begging bowl.
How lonely you must be
my poor bowl!

Off in the distance
frogs serenade
the rice fields.
This evening's
only song.

Summer evening,
the song of a cuckoo
rises from the mountain.
I dream of
the ancient poets.

Ryokan too
will fade like
the morning glories.
But his heart
will remain behind.

I lay down for a nap
in my tiny hut.
Frogs chant in the fields
and in the bamboo grove
the birds join in.

To find the Dharma,
drift east, west,
come and go,
give yourself
to the wind.

It's not that
I never walk
in the world of men:
I'm just better off
living alone.

You cuddled
and nursed him,
carried and cared for him,
but today you cremate his remains
in this desolate field.

Shall I draw water,
cut firewood,
or gather greens,
after the morning showers
let up.

In my begging bowl
violets and dandelions
mixed together;
an offering to the Buddhas
of the three worlds.

If the sleeves
of my black robe
were more ample
I'd shelter everyone
in this floating world.

Like trickling water
making its way
through mossy crevices,
I pass through this world
clear, transparent.

If people ask
how I live as a hermit,
I would respond:
I don't care if it rains
or the wind blows.

Fall

Remote villages
hidden in mist.
At twilight I return
toward home
surrounded by cedars.

Cold autumn night,
I wrap myself
in a white robe.
A bright clear moon
illuminates the sky.

If your hut
is secluded in the mountains
surely the moon,
wildflowers and maples
are among your friends.

Autumn fades,
mountains flaming red.
Ink ground,
sake poured
—still no one arrives.

Fall wind
grows colder
each day.
Voices of crickets
fewer, weaker.

Dew gathers
and it will be cold
on the mountain trail
—have one more cup
of sake before heading home.

On a journey,
each night I stay
in a different place
but my dream is the same,
a dream of home.

At dusk, I hike up slope
watching leaves fall fast,
my fingers numb
even though I warm
them in my sleeves.

The wind blows fresh
and moon shines clear:
let's dance all night
even if I am
getting old!

In the village
the music of
drums and flutes,
but here on the mountain
only wind in the pines.

Winter

In my small hut
showers of hail
strike a grove
of bamboo,
keep me awake.

Another blizzard
and the mountains are
deep with snow.
Any news from town
must wait for spring.

I lie down
near the hearth
and stretch out
but the cold it
goes right through me.

Who takes pity
on this old body?
At sunset I return
to retrieve the staff
I left behind.

Have you forgotten
the path to my hut?
Each evening I
await footsteps
but no one comes.

Evening,
the only conversation
on the mountain
is wind blowing
through pines.

Deep snow
in the mountains.
By what path
did you visit
in my dreams?

Asleep or awake
I yearn to take
the path of zen,
no matter
how hard.

An old man
shut inside all winter
deep in the mountains
—who would visit
except for you?

When I think
of the old days,
were they dreams or real?
Listening tonight
to the winter rain.

If they ask
what will Ryōkan
leave behind
as a deathbed poem
say *"Namu amida butsu."*

Deep snow outside
bundled up
in my solitary hut
I feel even my soul
slip away as dusk gathers.

SECTION 3

Dewdrops on a Lotus Leaf

A poetic dialog between Ryōkan and Teishin

Teishin's Essay on Ryōkan

Master Ryōkan was an heir of the Tachibana family in Izumosaki. When he was twenty-two he entered the monastery, and for years he studied under Sensei Kokusen, a virtuous priest of the Entsuji Temple in Tamashima, Bichu Province. Ryōkan also traveled far and visited well-known Zen masters, and continued his practice in several provinces for more than ten years until he reached his profound understanding.

Though he returned to his native province, he did not stay in one place but moved around until he finally settled on Kugami Mountain, where he lived and practiced for thirty years, drawing water and collecting firewood alone. Kimura, one of Ryōkan's students from Shimazaki who visited him to receive his teaching, felt uneasy about leaving the aging master alone so deep in the mountains and gently urged Ryōkan to move into a vacant cottage on his land. Overwhelmed by the proposal, Ryōkan could scarcely say no and moved into the offered cottage, comforted by his host's hospitality.

Six years later, in early spring, Ryōkan passed away. Though his life transcended this world he did not abandon his sense of beauty toward nature. He captured his feelings on many subjects and events in poetry written in both Japanese and Chinese.

Poetry was not his occupation, and he never received any formal training, but he expressed himself in poetry whenever his heart was touched by something. His mode of expression echoed ancient poetic rhythm. Without any formal training, his noble form and tonal eloquence were far above that of any secular poet.

Ryōkan wrote poems in a variety of forms, chanting them away spontaneously or playfully, according to his mood, sometimes with extraordinary results. His subjects weren't only the Buddha's teachings but fairy tales, such as the moon and the rabbit; a begging bowl; or a blank sheet of paper. Whenever we recite them, our hearts will be moved and purified. Those who love poetry will gain faith in their hearts if they have the opportunity to read Ryōkan, and it would be my greatest pleasure to offer that opportunity.

Indeed, it was a pity to see his poems scattered, buried away, and forgotten by people. After a long search, visiting many places, I was able to collect Ryōkan's poems within my reach. To this collection [Ryōkan's ninety-seven Japanese poems collected by Teishin are not included here] I added the poems we exchanged during the time I visited his cottage. It was my intention to have it with me as a keepsake so that I could repay my gratitude to him by reading it each morning and evening, remembering the past.

—the first day of May, sixth year of Tempo(1834)

—written by Teishin

Teishin

Hearing of the master's fondness for bouncing a ball,
I sent this poem with my ball

This is it:
playing ball is the Buddha's way;
no matter how long you bounce
you cannot exhaust
the depth of the Dharma.

Ryōkan

Try it, bounce
1,2,3,4,5,6,7...
up to ten
and begin again.
This is the way.

Teishin

When we first met:

Meeting you at last:
this joy and happiness
seem to be a dream
from which
I've not yet wakened.

Ryōkan

In this dream world,
while dozing,
we talk about a dream,
and we accept the dream
whenever it comes.

Teishin

After discussing the way, late into the night,
the master wrote this poem

Ryōkan

The sleeves
of my white cotton robe
cold in the autumn night,
above the moon
shining clear, expanding.

Teishin

Still I wanted to linger longer:

Looking up at the moon,
a thousand years and generations pass.
I want to watch
the sky-crossing moon,
though I hear no words.

Ryōkan

As long as our hearts,
are changeless,
like an ever-climbing vine,
we face the moon,
a thousand years and generations pass.

Teishin

After awhile I received his poem in a letter:

Ryōkan

Have you forgotten
or has the road hidden itself?
For days I have waited
passing the time
with no news from you.

Teishin

My poems in reply:

Because of worldly affairs
I have secluded myself
in a mole's hut.
Body and mind confused,
I am not free to come.

Although the moon
shines clearly along
the mountain's edge
thin clouds
obscure the peak.

Ryōkan

In the sky,
the moon
pure and clear,
shining through the void
from China to Japan.

The past and the present,
the false and the true are just
thin clouds which obscure
the mountain peak.
Shall we brush them away
revealing light?
What do you think, friend?

Teishin

In early spring I replied, inquiring about his health:

Day by day winter
recedes on itself.
and suddenly
without warning
spring arrives.

Waking,
there is neither
light nor darkness.
The moon at dawn
lights the dream road.

Ryōkan

More than any
mass of jewels and gold
filling this world, under heaven.
I treasure your letter
at the beginning of spring.

Following the Dharma way
there is nothing
to grasp in your hands
because it is,
as it is.

Teishin

Spring wind
melts the deep snow
on the mountain,
but along the rocks
the valley stream is still.

Ryōkan

If the deep snow
melts high on the mountains,
can it be long
before water is gushing
in the valley stream?

Teishin

Where did spring
come from I ask?
The plum blossoms
don't answer
but the warbler sings.

Ryōkan

Drifting like the
floating clouds,
when I hear
the cuckoo's song again
where shall I meet you?

When the autumn bush-clover
blossoms and flowers
come and see me.
If I'm still alive
we will celebrate together.

Teishin

Without waiting very long, I visited sooner

When autumn bush-clover
blossoms and flowers
is too long to wait.
As summer grasses open
I arrive.

Ryōkan

With the flowering
of autumn bush-clover too distant,
you push aside
the dewy summer grass
to visit me again!

Teishin

One summer day I visited, but the master had gone somewhere

Only a lotus blossom
arranged in a vase,
guardian of the hermitage,
its fragrance
filling the room.

Ryōkan

Nothing to look at
but a lotus blossom
arranged in a small vase.
Whenever you see this
remember me.

Teishin

A friend informed me Ryōkan was going to visit Yoita, and I rushed to visit him but found he was leaving the next day. As we talked among ourselves someone jokingly suggested we call our master "Crow" as it fit his dark complexion and black robes.

Our master said the name did fit him well and replied with this poem:

Ryōkan

Wherever I roam
on this journey
starting tomorrow
people will know me
by the name Crow.

Teishin

Mountain crow
whenever you travel
to villages and beyond,
take this young crow with you
even though her feathers are weak.

Ryōkan

'With my invitation
you are welcome
to come along.
but if people look suspicious
what should I do?

Teishin

A kite flys with a kite,
a sparrow with a sparrow,
a heron with a heron,
a crow with a crow.
Who would be suspicious?

Teishin

Ryōkan promised to visit my hermitage in fall, but he wrote that he was not well and hesitant to travel:

Ryōkan

The full blossoms
of the autumn bush-clover
have passed their prime.
Because of my illness
I am unable to keep my promise.

Teishin

Instead of feeling better, his health deteriorated when the winter came and according to a friend, he shut his door to visitors. I sent a poem with a letter:

Please endure
your condition:
even now
don't avoid
a moment's dream.

Teishin

For a time I heard no word and then a poem arrived:

Ryōkan

When spring returns
and the catalpa leafs out
         come quickly
from your grass hut.
I am eager to see you.

Teishin

Near the end of December I was informed that Ryōkan's condition had deteriorated. Shocked by the news I rushed to see him. Fortunately, sitting on his bed he looked peaceful, and seemed pleased to see me.

Ryōkan

When? When? I repeated,
waiting for you to come.
Now that you are here,
seeing each other,
what else have I to ask for.

Ryōkan

On the Musashi plain,
dew on the grass blades
lingers awhile
only to disappear;
not so with myself.

Teishin

Given the circumstances, I stayed by his side day and night, caring for
him and watching as he grew weaker day by day, without knowing what
to do. I feared he might pass away before long and was overcome with
sorrow.

Even for me who
should transcend
the border of life and death,
the great sorrow of parting
is still painful.

Ryōkan

Showing its underside,
showing its face
a falling maple leaf.

(he responded with this poem by another)

Teishin

The master murmured some haiku, a few I recall:

Ryōkan

Calm, autumn's arrival.
Here, the night rain falls
on the entire mountain.

The wind bell ringing
a couple of feet away
from the bamboo.

Visitors worry
whenever I feel
just a little sleepy.

Among the green leaves
white kobushi flowers
at their prime.

On rainy days
he really feels lonely
—this monk, Ryōkan!

The new pond,
a frog jumps in,
—no sound!

Ryōkan drew a picture of a skull and wrote:

Coming they beat,
going they strike,
—thoughts all night long.

Teishin

Distant waves
seem to come,
seem to go...

When I offered the above, immediately Ryōkan added this

Ryōkan

Clear and bright
your words and understanding.

My master died on January 6th in the second year of Tempo
(1831) at the age of 74.

—Teishin

I wrote to the honorable Seiri asking for his suggestions on what I should name this collection

Seiri replied:

Indeed,
we should regard
these as true jewels,
—dewdrops on a lotus leaf,
pierced and gathered together.

Dewdrops On A Lotus Leaf was compiled four years after Ryōkan's death. Forty-one years later, at 75, Teishin died and left as her farewell poem:

Distant waves
seem to come
seem to go.
So I have lived my life
leaving everything to the blowing wind.

THE TRANSLATORS

Dennis Maloney is a poet and translator. He is also the editor and publisher of the widely respected White Pine Press in Buffalo, New York. His works of translation include *The Stones of Chile* by Pablo Neruda, *The Landscape of Castile* by Antonio Machado, *Tangled Hair: Poems of Yosano Akiko* (with Hide Oshiro), *Dusk Lingers: Haiku of Issa*, *The House In The Sand* by Pablo Neruda and the forthcoming *The Poet and the Sea* by Juan Ramon Jimenez. A number of volumes of his own poetry have been published including *Sitting In Circles*, published in Japan in a bilingual edition, *The Pine Hut Poems*, and *The Map Is Not The Territory: Poems and Translations* (Unicorn Press, 1990).

Hide Oshiro is a Japanese visual artist living in the United States. He focuses on book art as a major component of his work. His visual art is includes a fully illustrated volume of Basho's travel journal, *Back Roads To Far Towns*, as well as an illustated volume of *Tangled Hair: Poems of Yosano Akiko.* He and Dennis Maloney have collaborated on a number of translation projects.

For Further Reading

Abe, Ryuichi & Haskel, Peter, *Great Fool: Zen Master Ryōkan*,
University of Hawaii Press, 1996.
Stevens, John, *One Robe, One Bowl: The Zen Poems of Ryōkan*,
Shambhala (Weatherhill), 1977
Stevens, John, *Dewdrops on a Lotus Leaf: Zen Poems of Ryōkan*,
Shambhala, 1993
Watson, Burton, *Ryōkan: Zen Monk—Poet of Japan*, Columbia
University Press, 1992

Companions for the Journey Series

Inspirational work by well-known writers in a small-book format
designed to be carried along on your journey through life.

Volume 20
Mountain Tasting
Haiku and Journals of Santoka Taneda
Translated by John Stevens
978-1-935210-03-0   200 PAGES $16.00

Volume 19
Between the Floating Mist
Poems of Ryokan
Translated by Hide Oshiro and Dennis Maloney
978-1-935210-05-4   90 PAGES $14.00

Volume 18
Breaking the Willow
Poems of Parting, Exile, Separation and Retun
Translated by David Lunde
978-1-893996-95-3   96 PAGES $14.00

Volume 17
The Secret Gardens of Mogador
Translated by Rhonda Dahl Buchanan
978-1-893996-99-1   240 PAGES $15.00

Volume 16
Majestic Nights
Love Poems of Bengali Women

Translated by Carolyne Wright and co-translators

978-1-893996-93-9   108 PAGES $15.00

Volume 15
Dropping the Bow
Poems from Ancient India
Translated by Andrew Schelling

978-1-893996-96-0   128 PAGES $15.00

Volume 14
White Crane
Love Songs of the Sixth Dali Lama
Translated by Geoffrey R. Waters

1-893996-82-4   86 PAGES $14.00

Volume 13
Haiku Master Buson
Translated by Edith Shiffert and Yuki Sawa

1-893996-81-6   256 PAGES $16.00

Volume 12
The Shape of Light
Prose Pieces by James Wright

1-893996-85-9   96 PAGES $14.00

Volume 11
Simmering Away: Songs from the Kanginshu
Translated by Yasuhiko Moriguchi and David Jenkins
Illustrations by Michael Hofmann

1-893996-49-2   70 PAGES $14.00

Volume 10

Because of the Rain: Korean Zen Poems
Translated by Won-Chung Kim and Christopher Merrill
1-893996-44-1   96 PAGES $14.00

Volume 9
Pilgrim of the Clouds
Poems and Essays from Ming Dynasty China
Translated by Jonathan Chaves
1-893996-39-5   192 PAGES $15.00

Volume 8
The Unswept Path: Contemporary American Haiku
Edited by John Brandi and Dennis Maloney
1-893996-38-7   220 PAGES $15.00

Volume 7
Lotus Moon: The Poetry of Rengetsu
Translated by John Stevens
Afterword by Bonnie Myotai Treace
978-1-893996-36-6   132 PAGES $14.00

Volume 6
A Zen Forest: Zen Sayings
Translated by Soioku Shigematsu
Preface by Gary Snyder
1-893996-30-1   120 PAGES $14.00

Volume 5
Back Roads to Far Towns: Basho's Travel Journal
Translated by Cid Corman
1-893996-31-X   94 PAGES $13.00

Volume 4
Heaven My Blanket, Earth My Pillow

Poems from Sung Dynasty China by Yang Wan-Li
Translated by Jonathan Chaves
1-893996-29-8   128 PAGES $14.00

Volume 3
10,000 Dawns: The Love Poems of Claire and Yvan Goll
Translated by Thomas Rain Crowe and Nan Watkins
1-893996-27-1   88 PAGES $13.00

Volume 2
There Is No Road: Proverbs by Antonio Machado
Translated by Mary G. Berg and Dennis Maloney
1-893996-66-2   118 PAGES $14.00

Volume 1
Wild Ways: Zen Poems of Ikkyu
Translated by John Stevens

1-893996-65-4   152 PAGES $14.00